Incredible Explorers

Samuel de Champlain
Exploring the Great Lakes

Zachary Anderson

Cavendish Square

New York

PPublished in 2015 by Cavendish Square Publishing, LLC
243 5th Avenue, Suite 136, New York, NY 10016

Library of Congress Cataloging-in-Publication Data

Anderson, Zachary.
Samuel de Champlain : exploring the Great Lakes / Zachary Anderson.
pages cm. — (Incredible explorers)
Includes index.
ISBN 978-1-50260-138-4 (hardcover) ISBN 978-1-50260-139-1 (ebook)
1. Champlain, Samuel de, 1574-1635—Juvenile literature. 2. Explorers—Great Lakes (North America)—Biography—Juvenile literature. 3. Explorers—North America—Biography—Juvenile literature. 4. Explorers—France—Biography—Juvenile literature. 5. Great Lakes (North America)—Discovery and exploration—French—Juvenile literature. 6. New France—Discovery and exploration—French—Juvenile literature. 7. North America—Discovery and exploration—French—Juvenile literature. I. Title.

F1030.1.A53 2015
910.92—dc23
[B]

2014030290

Editor: Andrew Coddington
Copy Editor: Cynthia Roby
Art Director: Jeffrey Talbot
Designer: Douglas Brooks
Photo Researcher: J8 Media
Senior Production Manager: Jennifer Ryder-Talbot
Production Editor: David McNamara

The photographs in this book are used by permission and through the courtesy of: Cover photo; Foundation of the city of Quebec by Samuel de Champlain in 1608, 1848 (oil on canvas), Garneray, Ambroise-Louis (1783-1857)/Archives-de la Manufacture, Sevres, France/Archives Charmet/Bridgeman Images; Boat Seal by Vector Lady; Joseph L. Pinsonneault/File:Samuel de Champlain No 23 (HS85-10-16077) original.tif/Wikimedia Commons, 4; The strangest sight the Prince of Wales saw in Canada: The arrival of Champlain on his ship (litho), Matania, Fortunino (1881-1963)/Private Collection/© Look and Learn/Peter Jackson Collection/Bridgeman Images, 6; Unknown, After Hieronino Custodis (fl. 1589–1598)/File:British - A Man, called Sir Martin Frobisher Kt - Google Art Project.jpg/Wikimedia Commons, 10; DEA/M. SEEMULLER/De Agostini Picture Library/Getty Images, 12; © North Wind Picture Archives, 14; © North Wind Picture Archives, 18–19; Trappers trading with Native Americans, New France (colour litho), Bombled, Louis Charles (1862-1927) (after)/Private Collection/© Look and Learn / Bridgeman Images, 22; © NorthWind Achives, 24; Samuel de Champlain/File:Samuel de Champlain Carte geographique de la Nouvelle France. jpg/Wikimedia Commons, 27; © North Wind Picture Archives, 30; Interim Archives/Archive Photos/Getty Images, 34; © North Wind Picture Archives, 36; Illustrations of Algonquin dress, engraving from Voyages of Sieur de Champlain by Samuel de Champlain (ca 1574-1635), 17th century (engraving), Champlain, Samuel de (1567-1635)/Private Collection/Bridgeman Images, 38; Wilkie, Robert D. (artist) and L. Prang & Co. (publisher)/File:Lake Champlain (Boston Public Library).jpg/Wikimedia Commons, 43; D. DEA/G. DAGLI ORTI/De Agostini Picture Library/Getty Images, 43; D. Gordon E. Robertson/File:Champlain statue, Nepean Point, Ottawa.jpg/Wikimedia Commons, 47; © North Wind Picture Archive, 49; Native American Algonquin Indian village of Pomeiock, Gibbs Creek, North Carolina, showing huts and longhouses inside a protective palisade. Sketch from observations made by English expedition under John White in 1585./Universal History Archive/UIG/Bridgeman Images, 50; Samuel de Champlain surrendering Quebec to Admiral Kirke, 20 July 1629 (colour litho) by English School, (20th century)/Bridgeman Images, 57.

Printed in the United States of America

Contents

Introduction
Exploring for France 4

Chapter 1
Champlain's Early Voyages 6

Chapter 2
Returning to the New World 14

Chapter 3
The Failed Colonies 22

Chapter 4
Setback in New France 30

Chapter 5
Taking Sides in a Local Conflict 36

Chapter 6
Strengthening New France 43

Chapter 7
Final Years in New France 49

Timeline 58

Glossary 60

For More Information 62

Index 63

Introduction

Exploring for France

Samuel de Champlain was a navigator, mapmaker, and explorer who played a key role in France's colonization of the **New World**, specifically what is now modern-day Canada. Representing France and King Henry IV, Champlain would not settle for just

Samuel de Champlain helped transform France's holdings in the New World from simple fur trading settlements to thriving colonies.

a fur-trading presence for his country in North America. He wanted to make Québec a powerful **colony**. In addition, Champlain, like many other explorers of the day, attempted to find the **Northwest Passage** to Asia. He forged alliances with many Native tribes and served as a missionary for Christianity in the new region.

Although he never found the riches of Asia, Champlain remained dedicated to establishing France's presence in North America, attempting to establish settlement after settlement and enduring the severe, sparse conditions there. He, like Jacques Cartier and other explorers before him, quickly became familiar with the isolation of life in the wilderness. Champlain survived largely by his cunning instincts and by trading with the Native people, sometimes from surplus provisions sent over from Europe. He also adopted many of the farming techniques that were used by the Native Americans.

Learning farming techniques from the Natives is just one way that Champlain worked with local tribes. Unlike many European explorers, Champlain forged alliances with a number of tribes, fighting the Native people only when he needed to support the tribes he had aligned with in their local rivalries. The Native people helped Champlain as he mapped the coasts, and Champlain learned and recorded what he learned about the local's culture and traditions. Over time, he and the French would use Native trade routes as the basis for the French's exploration of the northern portion of North America. However, Champlain's most lasting mark on North America was his role in the settlement of Québec, an original French outpost that remains to this day.

Chapter 1
Champlain's Early Voyages

S cholars agree that Samuel de Champlain was born in Brouage, a port town on the west coast of France in the province of Saintonge. For years, academics disagreed on the year of his birth. Some historians believed it occurred in 1567, while others

Since birth, Champlain seems to have been destined to become a great sailor and navigator.

thought it was 1570. Both camps were eventually proven wrong. Champlain's baptismal certificate was discovered in 2012, and the date on the document was August 13, 1574. His parents, as listed on the form, were Anthoynee Chapeleau and Margerite Le Roy. Champlain may have received his seafaring spirit from his uncle, who historians believe was a sea captain.

Brouage, where Champlain grew up, was an important seventeenth-century seaport as well as a center for the salt industry. Salt was the main mineral used to preserve meats and fish during that time. In fact, the harbor of Brouage was the first European place for trading salt, established as early as 1047, centuries before Champlain's birth. Today, however, Brouage is no longer on the waterfront because the sea has receded over time.

Like the other boys in his village, the young Champlain would have been taught how to read and write by the parish priest. Although there is no evidence about what his youthful interests were, or his mannerisms, it is safe to assume that he probably learned to sail and fish at an early age. Since Champlain developed into such an accomplished writer and a person with a gift for leadership and organization, we can assume that he enjoyed at least some of his schoolwork and was quick at learning his letters. His skills as a self-taught mapmaker show that he had a good eye for accurate drawing as well.

Champlain was a devout Catholic. In his books, he wrote about "the idolatry [worship of physical idols] of **paganism** [being] over-thrown, and Christianity proclaimed throughout all the regions of the earth," and he sincerely wanted to bring Christianity to the New World. He wrote, "I came to the conclusion that I would be doing very wrong if I did not work to find some means to bring [the Native peoples] to the knowledge of God." Champlain was far from a religious fanatic, though. He was a keen student of other cultures, most of the time objectively reporting what he had witnessed. He had a softer side as well, stating: "the thought of slavery brings tears to one's eyes."

Religious Wars

He may not have realized it in his seaport home of Brouage, but Champlain, was growing up during a very troubled period in France's history. The **Huguenots** were French Protestants, members of a church that began in France about fifteen years before Champlain's birth.

The Huguenots' beliefs put them at opposition with both the Catholic Church and the French Catholics. Since Catholicism was the ruling religion in France, the Huguenots were soon branded as heretics, or dissidents. Religious and political matters grew so bitter between the competing factions that, in 1562, more than a thousand Huguenots were massacred. This horrifying event started the Wars of Religion. As a young man, Champlain fought on the side of the Catholics under the command of Henry of Navarre, who later became King Henry IV of France. The conflicts, which raged throughout France until 1598, were ended when King Henry IV signed the Edict of Nantes.

Champlain's father must have set a strong example for his son, since as a boy Champlain sailed with his father on several short voyages. These sailing excursions probably helped Champlain familiarize himself with the navigational instruments of the day, which most likely included an **astrolabe**, a basic wooden or brass disk that marked various degrees north or south of the equator.

Champlain loved the art of navigation. He said, "[Navigation] has always seemed to me to occupy the first place. By this art we obtain a knowledge of different countries, regions, and realms ... This is the art ... which led me to explore the coasts of ... America, especially ... **New France**, where I have always desired to see the lily flourish." By the lily, he meant the *fleur-de-lys*, the flower that was the symbol of the French monarchy until the 1789 revolution. New France refers to northeastern Canada, particularly Québec.

The Tools of Navigation

A sailor finds longitude, the distance east or west of a generally accepted reference location, by comparing local shipboard time with the local time at a reference location, kept by a clock. While clocks existed in Champlain's day, they were inaccurate and almost useless while at sea. However, measuring latitude doesn't require clocks but depends on other instruments, such as the astrolabe, which determines latitude by measuring the angle between the horizon and Polaris, the North Star. Even today, navigation is based mostly on latitude and longitude. One of the most commonly accepted reference points is the Greenwich Observatory in England. Champlain must have also learned how to read a magnetic compass.

Champlain would have mostly relied upon dead reckoning. A navigator uses dead reckoning by starting at a known position, then measuring as accurately as possible the speed of the ship and of the ocean currents, as well as the ship's heading and downwind drift. Dead reckoning can be a very accurate method, although it's easy for errors to accumulate, often contributing to a misguided journey. To correct this, sailors must use reliable instruments as well as their own natural instincts of direction. Since seventeenth-century mechanical clocks weren't very accurate, mariners often used an hourglass to keep track of time. The most common were the half-hour and four-hour glasses. The ship's boy would be the one responsible for turning the first glass every half-hour, then calling out the time or hitting a bell to mark its passing. Every four hours, he would turn the four-hour glass. Many modern ships still use this four-hour system.

Champlain fought alongside famous English explorer Sir Martin Frobisher (above) during the war with Spain.

Fighting for France

Toward the end of the sixteenth century, there was a power struggle between Spain and France, as well as between Spain and England. The Spanish tried and failed to conquer England in 1588. Soon after, Champlain joined the Maréchal d'Aumont as one of King Henry IV's army commanders leading the fight to drive the Spanish out of France.

He soon became **quartermaster** of King Henry's cavalry and fought in the French army for four years. By 1594, Champlain was part of a joint French and English military effort and fought beside the famous English explorer Sir Martin Frobisher (1535–1594). Although Frobisher died in battle, Champlain managed to serve through four years of war unharmed. The war finally ended in 1598 with the signing of the Peace (or Treaty) of Vervins. King Henry's forces had won.

Samuel de Champlain

Once the war ended, Champlain was free to think about what he wanted to do next. He had already realized that the life of a soldier was not for him. Now in his late twenties, Champlain began hunting for a more suitable career, such as being a sea captain.

Heading Out On the High Seas

Champlain demonstrated his first true interest in the sea in 1598. It was during that year that he joined his uncle, Guillaume Hellaine, a known seafarer, for his first genuine voyage. Together they sailed to Spain aboard the *Saint Julien*, a French ship that had been chartered by the Spanish. Hellaine had been hired by the Spanish government to be the pilot general of the fleet, guiding the Spanish soldiers who had been in France back to their homeland. The voyage became a defining moment for the youthful Champlain, who was given the opportunity to take command of a ship and prove himself an able leader. He also learned how to speak with the sailors in their native Spanish tongue.

Toward the end of 1598, while he was still in the Spanish city of Seville, Champlain was offered a permanent post on the *Saint Julien*, possibly as commander or navigator. He was to sail to the West Indies and New Spain with the annual fleet that took goods to the colonies and brought New World goods back to Spain. Over two years, Champlain would sail the *Saint Julien* on several voyages throughout the Caribbean. These voyages clearly inspired the explorer in Champlain and would pique his curiosity about discovering new lands and bodies of water.

Champlain set sail on his first transatlantic journey in January 1599. Like most of his later transatlantic crossings, he reached his destination, this time the West Indies, without incident. While there, Champlain journeyed through the Caribbean Sea, visiting

Champlain would follow in the footsteps of past explorers, such as Jacques Cartier (above), in establishing French colonies in North America.

many of its islands on a trip that spanned two and a half years.

After sailing through the Gulf of Mexico, Champlain landed on the Mexican coast at the main Spanish-controlled port, San Juan de Ulúa, and traveled inland on foot as far as Mexico City. (This was about seventy years after Hernán Cortés and the conquistadors had conquered the Aztec Empire and imposed Spanish rule on Mexico.)

Champlain was truly fascinated by the New World and drew maps of the West Indies and Central America. He wrote, "[I] was amazed by the beauty of the temples, palaces, and great houses. I had not thought they would be so magnificent. The streets were so well laid-out, with fine big shops filled with goods of all kinds."

Champlain returned to his ship by way of Panama. It was the first time he observed the Isthmus of Panama, the narrow strip of land that separated the Caribbean Sea from the Pacific Ocean. Back aboard the *Saint Julien*, Champlain contemplated the idea of a canal through Panama to shorten sailing time. Remarkably, his idea, first proposed more than three centuries before, was very close to the actual **Panama Canal** today.

Champlain returned from the New World to Spain in March 1601. He had kept a journal of his explorations throughout the voyage through the West Indies and the Gulf of Mexico, and he offered it for publication when he returned to Europe. He had clearly been rushed in the writing and editing of the journal, since most of the illustrations he mentioned were actually missing. *Narrative of a Voyage to the West Indies and Mexico in the Years 1599–1602*, published first in French, wasn't translated to English until the nineteenth century.

While Champlain's first book was not a runaway bestseller, it did get him noticed by some very important and influential people. They took particular notice of the detailed maps Champlain had drawn of the islands and lands that he had visited. These maps began to build Champlain's reputation as a **cartographer** and explorer, as well as a writer. The New World maps that Champlain compiled prompted King Henry to install him as a royal geographer.

Chapter 2

Returning to the New World

C hamplain left Spain to return to his home country sometime in the first year or two of the seventeenth century. With his experience as a navigator and mapmaker from his first trip to the New World, Champlain had developed

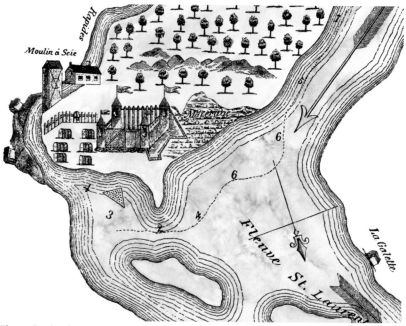

Champlain's talent as a cartographer helped get him noticed by King Henry IV. His skills in mapmaking and navigation would aid him in his own expeditions to the New World.

useful sailing skills, making him particularly valuable to many nations, including his homeland France, which was looking to explore and claim its own part of the New World. However, Champlain didn't want to be just a cartographer. He also knew he wasn't ready to settle down to a desk job. Champlain had been bitten by the bug of exploration during his travels to the New World. However, if he wanted to return to the New World, he would need to find a sponsor for subsequent voyages.

Sailing to New France

At last, Champlain had an idea. Once back in his homeland and eager to gain sponsorship for future explorations, he made several visits to the governor of Dieppe, Sieur (Lord) Commander Aymar de Chaste. The governor was a valiant old soldier whom Champlain had met on the battlefield while trying to drive the Spanish from France. Champlain also knew that King Henry, trying to promote trade in furs and fish from the New World, had granted de Chaste control of the territory between what are now the modern cities of Philadelphia and Montreal. Champlain was hoping to be assigned a mission from the sieur.

Sure enough, Champlain did eventually receive word through the governor's secretary that King Henry was supportive of his continued exploration of the New World, specifically the North American territory the French had claimed. This included lands that had been given to Sieur Commander de Chaste. King Henry hadn't given up on the idea of French colonies abroad, so the purpose of future exploration in the New World was to see how and where colonies could best be established. Henry IV no doubt remembered that Champlain had served the crown bravely and loyally during the earlier war against Spanish forces, and the king was one to repay it accordingly.

Champlain, it was agreed, was to sail with Francis Gravé, Sieur Du Pont, a merchant and fur trader whom he referred to as Pont Gravé. Champlain, by all accounts, got along famously with his partner. The agreement between the two men was for Champlain to see all that he could of the New World and basically command himself and his journeys. In other words, Champlain was being given approval to explore the lands and waterways freely, just as he had hoped.

EARLIER FRENCH ATTEMPTS AT EXPLORING THE NEW WORLD

Before Champlain's time, there had already been some attempts by the French to colonize the New World. In the middle of the sixteenth century, explorer Jacques Cartier (1491–1557) and Jean-François de la Rocque de Roberval (circa 1500–1560), a nobleman who was named viceroy of the proposed colony, had both tried to start colonies near and in what is now the modern city of Québec. Driven by their collective lust for gold, they both failed to find the riches they sought.

By 1541, Cartier and Roberval had been forced to abandon their prospecting projects as failures, finding only quartz and iron pyrite (commonly called fool's gold because of its resemblance to gold) instead of diamonds and gold. Roberval's mishandling of the situation, along with his poor leadership skills and Cartier's inability to settle among the Native peoples, contributed to the end of the expedition, which was poorly funded by the French. Instead, by the turn of the seventeenth century, several trading sites had been established along the Saint Lawrence River and the coast of Newfoundland, which before the expedition was thought to be a group of tiny islands. Most of the trading sites were at least 350 miles (563 kilometers) northeast of Québec. Much of inland North America still remained uncharted.

On March 15, 1603, Pont Gravé and Champlain set sail from France aboard Pont Gravé's ship, *La Bonne Renommée*, bound for the New World, specifically for the coast of what is now eastern Canada. Their voyage across the Atlantic Ocean was relatively uneventful, other than the occasional storm, but both men kept a watchful eye for icebergs.

They reached the Canadian coast in early May and anchored the ship at what is now Cape Diamond in Québec. From there, Pont Gravé and Champlain boarded a smaller boat, one that could manage the shallower waters of the Saint Lawrence River. They sailed down what has been called the Rivière de Canada (River of Canada), and by May 24 they anchored at the trading post of Tadoussac, a small port at the junction of the Saint Lawrence and Saguenay Rivers.

Champlain was, as he always had been, a keen observer of his surroundings. He noted that the country was mountainous, "full of woods of pine, cypress, fir trees, birch, and some other sorts of trees." His descriptions often included such fine details that they are considered the written equivalents to his finely drawn maps.

There had already been an earlier proposal by Jacques Cartier in 1535 for turning Tadoussac into a permanent settlement, but Champlain was not very impressed by what he saw there, particularly since Tadoussac had such a small harbor. He thought that where they had originally dropped anchor, back at the foot of Cape Diamond, would be the best site for a future French colony.

Also aboard the ship with the Frenchmen had been two Native Americans who had been in France as guests of the king. This led to Champlain experiencing the hospitality of the local tribe, men he ordinarily referred to in his writings as "savages." Historians have noted that despite Champlain's embrace of Native cultures, he also harbored some prejudices. In one passage of his accounts, the sagamore (subordinate chief) Anadabijou and perhaps more than eighty of his people welcomed the French to a feast. At this time one of the "savages" who had been to France gave a speech about how well he had been treated and how the French would protect them against their enemies, the **Iroquois**. After the speech ended, Anadabijou and the others shared a pipe of peace. Champlain wrote a complete description of the *tabagie*, or feast, that followed, which included moose, bear, seal, beaver, and a great deal of wild fowl. While the food itself was plentiful

and hearty, Champlain found the habit the Native people had of cleaning grease from their hands by running them through their hair or wiping them on the backs of dogs less than appealing.

Exploring the Area

Pont Gravé had come to Tadoussac primarily because of his trading business, while Champlain wanted only to explore. Still, probably because their relationship was a good one, Champlain persuaded Pont Gravé to travel with him.

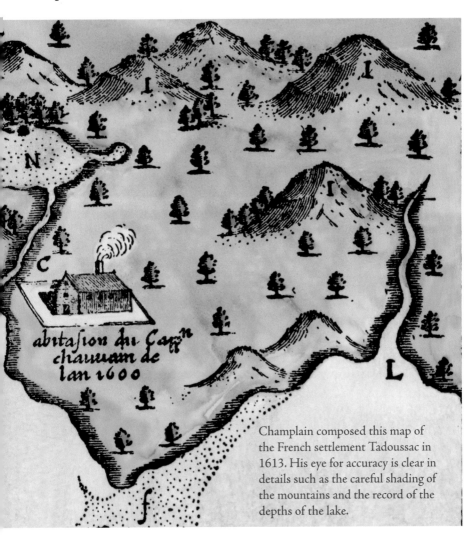

Champlain composed this map of the French settlement Tadoussac in 1613. His eye for accuracy is clear in details such as the careful shading of the mountains and the record of the depths of the lake.

They headed upriver in what Champlain described in his journals as "a very light little boat with five sailors," since the ship they had used before was too large and heavy for the smaller rivers where they meant to sail. Champlain might already have hoped that this was the river that could bring him closer to present-day Hudson Bay, a waterway he believed might run right through North America to Asia, the famed and fabled Northwest Passage.

This isn't as strange a concept as it might sound in these modern days of a well-mapped world. In 1603, no one yet knew just how large North America might be, or even whether it was a solid mass of land or merely a series of islands. A water route due west would have made an excellent shortcut to Asia.

Soon, however, to Champlain's disappointment, his search was halted by the fierce power of the Saint Louis Rapids, which lie near what is now Montreal. As Champlain said in his journal, "[I]t was so raging and interspersed with rocks that we found ourselves obliged to go . . . by land to see the upper part of the rapids."

Once they had climbed up to the top of the rapids, however, they met with further disappointment. There didn't seem to be any way or path to continue. By this point, Champlain's frustration was clear. He wrote, "All that we could do was to note the difficulties; the whole country; the length of this river; the reports of savages as to what was in the land; their accounts of the people; the places; the sources of the principal rivers, especially of the great Saint Lawrence River. Then I wrote a short account, and made an exact map of all I had seen and observed, and so we returned to Tadoussac, having made but little progress."

Frustrated though Champlain might have been, he did draw accurate maps of the region. He gained useful information about Lake Erie and Lake Ontario, the Detroit River, possibly Niagara Falls, and the rapids of the Saint Lawrence. And, though he didn't realize the advantage at the time, Champlain had been given his first chance to study a region that intrigued him enough to encourage his eventual return.

After sailing back to Tadoussac from upriver, Champlain found that the trading mission was completed. He and Pont Gravé then set sail from the New World in August and returned across the Atlantic Ocean to a safe anchor in France by year's end. His second book, *Of Savages, or Voyage of Samuel de Champlain, of Brouage*, made to New France in the year 1603, was published at that time.

The Mythical Northwest Passage

Champlain wasn't alone in trying to find the elusive Northwest Passage, the freshwater shortcut to Asia. In fact, for fifty years, other explorers from England, Spain, and France had been hunting for it, too. One of them had been the man whom Champlain had once fought beside in the war against Spain, Sir Martin Frobisher. Frobisher began searching for the northern waterway in 1576. Another was Champlain's contemporary, Henry Hudson, an Englishman sailing for the Dutch in 1607. All the expeditions failed, of course, since without planes or aerial photography no one could determine that such a water passage did not exist. It would take sailing south, as Magellan did a few decades after Champlain's initial voyage, for a European to make it to Asia by sailing west from Europe.

Champlain's second voyage to the New World had been a success, and it's likely that he was already contemplating returning to continue his explorations. However, upon his return to France, there was a complication, as Champlain's sponsor, Sieur Aymar de Chaste, had recently passed away. Champlain was going to have to find someone new to fund his voyages.

Chapter 3
The Failed Colonies

After the passing of Sieur Aymar de Chaste, things could have become complicated for Champlain. Luckily for him, the New World fur trade was too important and too lucrative for France. The wealthy throughout Europe

The earliest French settlements in the New World were little more than trading posts where French fur trappers traded with Native Americans.

loved wearing fur, and the unique coats of beavers were a very popular choice at the time. The French wanted the flow of **pelts** to continue uninterrupted. King Henry IV assigned the rights to the fur trade to Pierre du Gua, the Sieur de Monts.

De Monts, who had come to King Henry's attention through his bravery in fighting for France, was a natural choice for the distinction. As soon as the king rewarded him with a trading license, de Monts coordinated a company of merchants. In exchange for the king granting his company exclusive trading rights, de Monts was to establish French colonies in the New World and support them until they were self-sufficient.

However, there were many independent fur traders who didn't think too highly of a monopoly that sought to take away their livelihoods. The discontent of these men would fester and grow, and would lead to trouble in a short time.

As it happened, de Monts was a Huguenot (French Protestant) or, as Champlain said of him, someone "of the so-called reformed religion," but that didn't stop the two men from agreeing to work together on a new expedition and to remain friendly. In 1604, Champlain and de Monts sailed to the New World aboard Pont Gravé's ship, *La Bonne Renommée*. Pont Gravé was in command of a second ship in the three-ship fleet.

Champlain was in agreement with de Monts's decision that Tadoussac and the rocky land around it held few promises for permanent settlement or exploration. Instead, they landed farther southeast out in the Atlantic Ocean on Sable Island on May 1, 1604, in what Champlain called Acadie, or Acadia.

Verrazano and Acadia

Acadie, or in English, Acadia, was named by an earlier explorer, the Italian Giovanni da Verrazano, who had sailed up and down

Florentine explorer Giovanni da Verrazano (above) first discovered Sable Island, or Acadie, as Champlain called it, seventy-five years before Champlain. Champlain believed the island might contain the Northwest Passage.

the Atlantic coast and into the mouth of New York Bay about seventy-five years before Champlain. Verrazano was actually thinking of the shores of North Carolina when he applied the name, since that region reminded him of the Arcadia of ancient Greece. Unfortunately, sixteenth-century mapmakers weren't always working with accurate data. They labeled the territory of Acadia farther and farther northeast, until the name applied to Nova Scotia and Maine.

Verrazano, incidentally, had both a site, the Verrazano Narrows, and a bridge named in his honor centuries after his sixteenth-century death. In 1954, the Verrazano Narrows Bridge officially opened, connecting the New York City boroughs of Brooklyn and Staten Island.

Champlain theorized that Acadia, full of islands and waterways, might well hold a more promising chance of leading to a Northwest Passage. He was about to discover that this wasn't true. It was far from a pleasant place to stay, with bitter winters and savage winds. Today, the only inhabitants of Sable Island are sea birds, sea lions, and small, wiry, wild ponies, descendants of those brought by colonists who didn't remain, plus a rotating team of meteorologists.

A Difficult Winter

Sailing along the rugged coast of Nova Scotia, Champlain and de Monts finally decided that they would attempt to build a settlement on what de Monts named the island of Sainte-Croix. The island lies in the Saint Croix River, which separates New Brunswick from the United States. That winter, though, was brutal. By 1605, nearly half the colonists had died from infection or **scurvy**, a disease that is caused by a severe lack of vitamin C, and the site was abandoned. Champlain listed the symptoms of scurvy with scientific accuracy. He wrote of the settlers' bleeding gums, missing teeth, painful limbs, and small raised spots that resembled bites from fleas. He even had a chance to dissect some of the dead and discovered that scurvy destroyed internal organs as well.

At this point, Champlain wasn't certain about his comrade's wisdom. He later wrote in his journal, "Now, since Sieur de Monts did not wish to go to live on the Saint Lawrence River, he ought to have sent someone to explore a place suitable for the foundation of a colony, which would not be likely to be abandoned . . . There is no doubt at all that the soil . . . would have induced settlers to stay there. [Then] the English and the Flemish would not have got the benefit of places that they took from us, where they have settled to our loss."

Champlain, with what could be called flawless foresight, was referring to the English settlement of New England and the

Dutch settlement of New Amsterdam created about forty years later, in what is now New York City.

That spring, *La Bonne Renommée* moved farther along the rocky, foggy coast, with Champlain and de Monts still searching for a place for a colony to be located.

This gave Champlain a chance to fully explore the jagged coastline as far south as Cape Cod, making careful surveys and drawing maps as he went throughout the spring and summer of 1605. As always, he made detailed observations about everything he saw. For instance, he commented that Cape La Have, now a part of Nova Scotia, was "a place where there is a bay containing several islands covered with firs, and a great tract of oaks, young elms, and birches." Champlain identified dozens of birds and animals as well, from magpies to "sea wolves," most likely an older name for sea lions. Some of the names he gave to the places he visited are still in use, such as the Seal Islands, which lie off the coast of Nova Scotia.

On July 16, 1605, Champlain had a chance to discuss geography with some of the local Native peoples. He described sighting several of them who "danced on the beach" upon greeting him.

After sailing on in a west-southwest direction, Champlain finally dropped anchor near an island, ironically, in present-day Boston Harbor, a settlement that only twenty-five years later (1630) was settled by the Massachusetts Bay Company and thrived for the English. Still, it was never a location that Champlain believed would make an appropriate French colony.

Although sailing the seas off the coast of maritime Canada and New England could not have been easy, with its rough waters and risks of hidden rocks, Champlain wrote almost nothing about navigating its waters. Or perhaps he thought it far more important to describe and map only the land and its people.

Throughout his travels in the New World, Champlain was construct-
ing exceptionally detailed and accurate maps. This one of New France
describes the land's shape, features, Native peoples, flora, and more.

Early Accurate Maps

Professional cartographers, not explorers, usually drew maps in
the seventeenth century. Since these cartographers depended upon
information from explorers, navigators, and cosmographers, much
of that information was sometimes quite inaccurate. Some of the
sites on their maps, including entire islands, didn't actually exist.

Champlain, however, based his maps entirely on his own exploration
and observations, which included his interviews with Native people who
were familiar with the land and its formations and waterways. Since
he also used his own mathematical calculations, his maps were very
accurate. During the harsh winters of the years between 1604 and 1607,
Champlain drew sixteen detailed maps of North America, along with
accurate written descriptions of the people native to the area.

Champlain's maps are still treasured to this day. In 2008, famous
British auction house Sotheby's put up for auction a map that Champlain
made of Canada in 1612. The detailed map, which was the first printed
map to present factual representation of the Saint Lawrence River and
the Great Lakes, was expected to sell for as much as $75,000. However,
the officials significantly underestimated how valuable this historical
document of the early history of Canada would be. After the aggressive
bidding by several interested parties, the map sold for $235,000—more
than triple their original estimate!

Pleasant relations with the Native peoples continued. Near what is now Gloucester, Massachusetts, Champlain described a port that he named Le Beauport, or the Beautiful Harbor. It was here that he recounted another friendly meeting in which both sides enjoyed each other's company so much that they didn't want to part ways.

However, Champlain's main mission was to select a new site for a French colony. In the summer of 1605, an area was finally chosen, near La Baye Francoise, or what is now the Bay of Fundy, singled out partly because it was sheltered by a natural harbor, and also because there was a good source of freshwater nearby. Port-Royal, as it was named, was controlled by Champlain's friend Pont Gravé.

At first, everything seemed fine, and it looked as though the colony of Port-Royal was going to be a success. Champlain had served as an army quartermaster and understood just how bleak barracks life could be, especially in remote regions. He also knew that making a lively ritual out of mealtimes would improve the health and morale of his companions.

"We spent this winter very pleasantly," Champlain wrote, "and had good fare by means of the Order of Good Cheer which I established, and which everybody found beneficial to his health, and more profitable than all sorts of medicine we might have used. This Order consisted of a chain, which we used to place with certain little ceremonies about the neck of one of our people, commissioning him for that day to go hunting. The next day it was conferred upon another, and so on in order. All competed with each other to see who could do the best, and bring back the finest game. We did not come off badly." The early French settlers had finally found pleasant methods of survival.

A Colony Lost to the English

Port-Royal was reestablished as a French colony in 1610, a time of active hostility between the French and the English. As a result of this conflict, the English burned it down in 1613. Today, the ruins of Port-Royal, the first French colony in the New World, are a Canadian historic site, as well as a modern town. Excavations there have given us clues as to how the colonists lived. For instance, we know that they used pottery for dishes and food storage, and fragments of broken glass show that they had some luxury items, too, such as fragile wine glasses.

The British were not the only threat to de Monts, Champlain, and the other colonists. Independent fur traders, derisively referred to as "Basque interlopers" by Champlain (Basque is the region between France and Spain), had been trading on the coastline around the Gulf of Saint Lawrence for years. While de Monts had the legal right to all trading, he did not have the means to prevent the independent traders. His three-ship fleet could only cover so much of the coastline. There were also challenges back in France. The merchants that were not part of de Monts' company also wanted to profit from the spoils of the fur trade, and used the French courts to challenge Sieur de Monts' monopoly. In 1607, de Monts learned that the challenge had been successful, and that he had lost his monopoly. Without the funds to fight legal battles in France and territorial battles in the New World, de Monts, Champlain, and the colonists decided to return to France.

Chapter 4
Setback in New France

Despite the latest setback to de Monts and his fur trading monopoly, Champlain still was focused on returning to the New World, where he would establish a colony for France. He appealed to de Monts by reminding his

Québec City, founded by Champlain in 1608, is situated on the banks of the Saint Lawrence River. It became a primary foothold for the French in the New World, and it remains a bustling city today.

partner that the Saint Lawrence River would still be a crucial route in the fur trade. Champlain argued that to maximize the effectiveness of such a trade route, France needed a colony in the New World—one that would serve as a permanent settlement, as opposed to a trading post.

With that, he won his case. Champlain and his old comrade, Pont Gravé, were sent back across the Atlantic Ocean on this new mission of settlement on April 13, 1608. There were three ships in their fleet, all of which had been provided by de Monts. One ship, *Le Levrier*, was commanded by Pont Gravé and had Tadoussac as its destination. A second ship, *Le Don de Dieu*, commanded by Champlain, was tasked with the specific goal of locating a suitable settlement site. While the name of the third vessel went unrecorded, it was important because it served as a supply ship, carrying provisions for the transatlantic journey and the new settlement.

At this point, Champlain must have been comfortable crossing the Atlantic Ocean. Although it took months to reach the New World, the conditions aboard a cramped ship were far from pleasant, and there were never any guarantees of actually reaching North America. However, by the seventeenth century, it was no longer considered unusual for someone to make the crossing. Champlain, for his trouble, may have eventually set what was probably a record of twenty-two crossings as he tried to keep settlements funded and the French government interested in them.

Once again, Champlain had an uneventful journey, reaching the New World on May 26 and arriving at Tadoussac by June 3.

Once there, he had a shock. The Basques still hadn't surrendered to the idea of de Monts's monopoly. Pont Gravé, who had arrived before Champlain, was being held hostage by the hostile mountain dwellers.

This was where Champlain proved his skills as a natural diplomat. We don't have his speech to the angry Basques, but it must have been impressive because he managed to talk them into both releasing Pont Gravé and backing down from attacking the expedition.

After that narrow escape, Champlain and Pont Gravé continued up the Saint Lawrence River, hunting for a worthwhile place for a settlement. Champlain had learned from the Native people about a large inland waterway.

Though he didn't know it, this was not a sea, as the Natives had implied, but an enormous bay, later known as Hudson Bay after Henry Hudson, another explorer who would later perish there in 1611 while also searching for the Northwest Passage. Champlain wanted very much to see the bay, but as he stated, "I have often wished to make this discovery, but I have not been able to do it without the savages, who have been unwilling to have me or any other of our men go with them. Nevertheless, they have promised me that I shall go."

The Native people may have promised it, but they never did take him there. It is possible that the Natives were starting to regret showing the Europeans so much land because they would eventually claim it for their home nations.

Ideal Land

At last, on July 3, Champlain and Pont Gravé came to a region that the local **Algonquin** people called Québec. Champlain surveyed the area, hunting for the most suitable places for buildings. He said in his journal, he "could not find any more convenient or better situated than the point of Québec." In fact, Champlain liked it so much that he decided the settlement would become his new home.

Not everyone was pleased about the idea of a settlement, or with Champlain himself. Not long after his arrival in the area, Champlain was shocked to learn of a plot to assassinate him. One of the conspirators, Antoine Natal, thought better of it and confessed the plan. The ringleader of the plot was Jean Duval, a locksmith with links to the Basques as well as others who opposed de Monts's monopoly. In fact, the idea had been to first kill Champlain, then turn over Québec to the Basques.

The would-be assassins, four in all, were quickly found guilty. Duval was hanged, his head removed and mounted on a spike overlooking the settlement, and the remaining three were sent back to France. Afterward, there were no further plots.

What did remain was the amount of work that had to be finished. As Champlain wrote in his journal: "I immediately employed some of our workmen in cutting [some of the trees] down, in order to put our buildings there. Some I set to sawing boards, some to digging a cellar and making ditches, and others I sent to Tadoussac with the boat to get our supplies. The first thing that we made was the storehouse in which to put our provisions under cover."

Champlain frequently asked the Native Americans he encountered to lead him to Hudson Bay (pictured above), which he thought contained the passage to Asia.

Champlain also got the men to begin clearing the ground for gardens in which settlers could sow their grain, and he was pleased to see how fertile the soil seemed. There were Native settlements nearby, but that didn't bother him—he offered the people no trouble, and they, in turn, offered him none. In fact, Champlain liked the **Montagnais** Tribe and found them an attractive people, describing them as "well-built, without deformity, and ... active." He noted the clever way they got around over the snow on wide shoes made of woven branches. Champlain had never seen snowshoes before, and he was amazed at the way they allowed people to travel so easily over snow and ice. He also found the Montagnais a wary folk, since they found it difficult to rest at night for fear of being surprised by enemies. Whenever they thought they would be attacked, they would send their women and children to safety in Québec's

Samuel de Champlain

growing fort. Champlain allowed this, but he couldn't under-stand why they refused to accept his concept of a nightly watch.

The year passed, and by October, Champlain had seen the winter wheat and rye safely planted. All looked well. That winter turned into a severe one, though, clearly worse than normal, with cold and snow that completely isolated the new settlement from the world. Many of the settlers grew ill and died of scurvy.

The Montagnais fared no better. They, too, had been caught off-guard by the winter's severity, and many of them were near starving. Pitying them, especially the babies, Champlain did what he could to give them food and shelter. To his horror and disgust, he even saw the starving people try to eat a dog's rotted carcass. He wished they would learn how to farm and "take the trouble to sow Indian corn" so that they would have a year-round source of food.

The winter, and the resulting famine, finally ended. Champlain was pleased to see the variety of crops growing, noting that the land around Québec was "beautiful and pleasant, and [brought] all sorts of grains and seeds to maturity." He also noted the variety of fruits, herbs, and roots in the area, and felt that the colonists would be able to live off the fish and game that could be caught as well. Having survived a first brutal winter, it seemed as if Québec would become a cornerstone of New France.

Chapter 5

Taking Sides in a Local Conflict

S urviving the harsh winter, Champlain and his colonists had formed a bond with the local Montagnais tribe. As the two groups worked together, Champlain learned that the tribe was allied with other local tribes, but also had enemies

Champlain formed a close relationship with the Algonquin tribes in the region. He even fought alongside the Native Americans during the wars with their rivals.

as well. Like the French, Spanish, and English dispute over the land throughout the New World, two factions of Native tribes were each claiming the territory west of Québec. The Montagnais were part of the Algonquin group that was battling the Iroquois people for the land.

What Champlain and the French probably didn't realize is that the word "Algonquin" designated several Native nations sharing a common language. The French may not have understood just how complicated the situation was in the northeastern region of North America. They were now inhabiting the lands of several closely related peoples: the Micmac, the Montagnais, the Algonquin, the Attikamek, the Nipissing, the Abenaki, the Ottawa, and the Ojibwa.

The Iroquois Confederacy

The territory the Algonquin were claiming was also being claimed by another group of Native Americans: a union of several tribes called the Iroquois Confederacy. The Iroquois were far from the vicious enemy "savages" of Champlain's descriptions. Among other things, they were the creators of North America's first democratic union.

Some scholars date the Iroquois Confederacy (also known as the Iroquois League) to 1390 CE or even earlier, though others state that it was conceived around 1450–1500. At any rate, historians agree that it was a local creation, not something influenced by European ideas. The Confederacy consisted of the Mohawk (People of the Flint), the Onondaga (People on the Hills), the Seneca (Great Hill People), the Oneida (Granite People), and the Cayuga (People at the Mucky Land). In 1715, a sixth nation was also added, the Tuscarora (Shirt-Wearing People).

Like his maps, Champlain also made detailed illustrations of the Native Americans he interacted with. This particular illustration captures the style of dress for the Algonquins.

The Lake that Took Champlain's Name

Lake Champlain flows north from Whitehall, New York, bordering New York State and Vermont, across the U.S.-Canadian border to its outlet at the Richelieu River in Québec, more than 120 miles (193 km) away. From there, it joins the Saint Lawrence River, which eventually spills into the Atlantic Ocean. About 12 miles (19 km) wide and 400 feet (122 meters) deep, it holds over seventy islands and five distinct areas: the South Lake, the Main Lake (or Broad Lake), Malletts Bay, the Inland Sea (or Northeast Arm), and Missisquoi Bay.

Lake Champlain may also, like Scotland's Loch Ness, contain its own "monster," named Champ. Champlain himself reported seeing a creature the Native peoples called Chaousaron, but while his report is as detailed as he could make it, the creature was nothing more than a large garfish. Impressed by its size, Champlain eventually sent its skeletal remains to the king as a gift. However, people are still looking for evidence of Champ. In 2005, a pair of fishermen recorded a video of what they thought could possibly by Champ. While the news ran the story, and had forensic experts verify the authenticity of the video, many still scoff at the idea of Champ's existence.

The tension between the Iroquois Confederacy and the Algonquin made for an unstable situation for the new settlement of Québec, and the French feared that fighting between the Native Americans would ruin their dream of a profitable fur trade.

In July 1609, Champlain, who had been hearing his trading partners complain about the Iroquois, decided to join his Montagnais friends in an expedition against them. Joining up with a mixed group of Algonquians and **Hurons**, the party traveled up the Sorel River in Champlain's ship until they arrived at the Chambly Rapids. Here, Champlain and the others left the larger ship and continued by canoe.

In his travels, Champlain also described climbing high mountains. This is where, as he put it, "we were to meet our enemies."

Soon after, he and the Native people met up with a large force of the Iroquois on the north end of the lake. Both sides landed and put up barricades of trees. On the following day, they engaged in battle, and the Iroquois were defeated. This was primarily due to the fact that this was a battle fought with French firearms, something never before experienced by the tribe. Champlain killed two of the Iroquois chiefs with his **matchlock gun**, an early form of musket, and mortally wounded a third.

Even after the battle, Champlain thought the lake he had just crossed was one of the most spectacular and fascinating that he had seen. In fact, he was so impressed that he named the lake after himself. Today, it is still known as Lake Champlain.

After the battle, Champlain was shocked to see his Native allies torture one of their prisoners. Even though he recorded the entire procedure as unemotionally as possible, including the honor granted the prisoner for his bravery, he added with clear relief that he was able to give the man a merciful death with a quick shot from his musket. Champlain stated several times that he would have been pleased to see the Native peoples become Christian, and he sounded genuinely concerned about their well-being. Biased against the Iroquois as he was, thanks to his Montagnais friends, Champlain seemed to have understood something many of his contemporaries did not: Different people have different cultures.

Soon after this first French-assisted victory, the Huron people signed their first trade agreement with Champlain.

Then, in 1610, Champlain took part in another battle against the Iroquois, this time against one of their forts. Champlain described it as "made of heavy trees set close together in a circle, which is the usual shape of their fortresses."

During the attack, Champlain was wounded. An arrow slit the end of his ear and entered his neck. This must have been painful, but he was able to pull the arrow free and was self-possessed enough to note that it "was barbed on the end with a very sharp stone." Champlain wrote in his journal, "Nevertheless, my wound did not prevent me from doing my duty, nor our savages from doing their part; and likewise the enemy. The arrows were seen flying from one side and the other as thick as hail. The Iroquois were astonished at the noise of our muskets, and especially at the fact that the balls pierced better than their arrows."

Once again, the more advanced weaponry of the French was the deciding force in the battle. After they had destroyed this fortification, the French forced the Iroquois farther south and opened the upper Saint Lawrence River area to French trade.

No one seems to have understood that by forcing the Iroquois away from the Saint Lawrence, the French were sending them to trade directly with their English and Dutch rivals. Champlain also failed to realize that the English could, and did, sympathize with the Iroquois. He also didn't know that this opening battle was eventually going to instigate a war, with the French and their Algonquin allies against the English and the Iroquois.

Fighting the French and Indian War

The Anglo-French war dated from 1754 to 1763 and was actually part of the land struggle between Great Britain and France. While Europeans were barely aware of what was going on in the New World, the settlers in Canada and America were in the middle of what must have seemed like one long battle, complete with tribal warfare. Some historians believe it was then that the British colonies, on their own for much of the conflict, began to understand the need for an independent nation.

This war with the Iroquois and their English allies was not the only trouble Champlain had to deal with. The king of France, Henry IV, passed away. Champlain did not know how this would affect the colonies of New France. Would Henry's successor still put as much importance on maintaining a permanent post in the New World? Needing answers, Champlain decided to return to France.

Chapter 6

Strengthening New France

A fter returning to France in 1610, Champlain learned that his old partner, de Monts, was still willing to back the colony in New France for at least one more year. While Champlain was probably looking for a longer-term

The death of Champlain's sponsor King Henry IV (above) prompted him to leave his settlements in New France and return to Europe.

commitment, the year would give him more time to convince the rest of France how important it was for the country to establish a colony (or colonies) in the New World.

He also had problems of another nature on his mind. While Samuel de Champlain had an honorable reputation, he was now a single man at forty years of age. The Native tribes found this fact surprising, too, since he didn't even flirt with their women. Granted, his explorations and frequent trips to and from the New World had occupied most of his life. He was no longer a young man, though. It was high time for him to get married.

The society in which Champlain lived was not one that considered romantic love important. If there was any sort of courtship for Champlain, it must have been very brief indeed because in 1611, during his visit to France, he married Hélène Boullé, who was the daughter of Nicholas Boullé, a royal secretary. However, there was a slight complication. At the time of their wedding, Hélène was just a girl, only twelve years old.

It wasn't that her youth at the time of the marriage was so strange. Wide differences between the ages of husbands and wives weren't all that unusual in Champlain's day. In fact, for several hundred years in Western Europe, it had been the custom for a man to be much older than his wife, often by a decade or more.

Still, it was not considered proper for a marriage to be consummated until a wife had legally come of age. And so, according to the marriage settlement Champlain made, Hélène was to remain with her parents for another two years. It would not be until after that time passed that the marriage would be honored. As it happened, though, Madame Champlain stayed in France for a full ten years.

Founding Montreal

Champlain, meanwhile, returned to the New World in 1611 and continued his exploration of the Saint Lawrence region. Seventy-five years earlier, explorer Jacques Cartier had come upon the low peak there that is known as Mount Royal. Within a short distance of Mount Royal, Champlain found a site that he thought was perfect for a new settlement. He ordered that the ground be cleared and prepared for building, and he called the site La Place Royale. Place Royale is now part of downtown modern Montreal, and the low mountain called Mount Royal is now within the city's limits.

Across from Place Royale, an island lies in the Saint Lawrence River. Champlain, in a moment of romance or pride, named it Sainte-Hélène in honor of his young wife, who had yet to come to the New World. He wasn't at ease about the less-than-stable source for continued funding for New France and his own exploration of North America. At last he felt it necessary to return to France that same year, 1611, to see what he could learn.

When Champlain arrived in France, he found, as he had probably suspected, that de Monts had steadily lost his influence at the royal court after the death of King Henry IV. Those merchants who had once been interested in colonization now announced that they no longer wished to invest in the project.

Champlain immediately went to work hunting for a new sponsor. During this time, the man who had made so many transatlantic crossings without harm; who thought nothing of an arrow wound in the neck was brought down by "a wretched horse" that fell on him and nearly killed him while en route to Fountainbleau in France. This he recounted in his journal. Recuperating from his injuries in an inn, Champlain was trapped in confinement for weeks, unable to resume his search until later that year. This setback and recovery time must have seemed like an eternity to so active a man.

Champlain received some unexpected news. His teenage bride seemed to have grown tired of waiting for him. Even so, the new Madame Champlain, who was not quite fifteen years old, wasn't ready to leave France for life in the wilderness.

Meanwhile, back on his feet and active once more, Champlain managed to persuade the Count de Soissons to take an interest in New France. The count obtained a commission on October 8, 1612, that appointed him as governor of New France, with Champlain as his lieutenant-general. Champlain kept that office even though the Prince de Condé gained the rights of de Soissons soon after.

The year 1613 also saw the publication of Champlain's book *The Voyages of the Sieur de Champlain of Saintonge, Captain in ordinary for the King in the Navy, 1613.*

Still Searching for the Northwest Passage

Not long after his appointment, Champlain sent several ships back to New France to continue the colonization efforts. Toward the end of 1613, he again made the crossing himself.

Once back in the New World, Champlain set out from Sainte-Hélène on May 27 with four Frenchmen and a Native American to explore the region above Sault Saint Louis. His primary goal was to explore the Ottawa River. An interpreter, Nicolas de Vignau, had assured Champlain that he knew the way to "the sea of the North," meaning Hudson Bay. In 1613, people still hadn't given up hope of finding that elusive Northwest Passage. Many thought that the large body of water we now know as the Hudson Bay opened into the Pacific Ocean.

ASTROLABE LAKE

An astrolabe is an important device for sailors and navigators. They use it to track the position of heavenly bodies like the sun, moon, planets, and stars in order to calculate latitude. There's no doubt that Champlain would consider his astrolabe crucial and take it within him wherever he explored in the New World, particularly with his penchant for recording exact details of all his journeys.

At one point, while portaging over the pile of logs clogging the shore of Green Lake, Champlain lost his astrolabe. The lake, tradition has it, was later renamed Astrolabe Lake in memory of the incident. Then, more than 200

Champlain lost his valuable astrolabe in Green Lake, which was later called Astrolabe Lake. The astrolabe was recovered over 200 years later and is now on display in a museum.

years later, in 1867, a fourteen-year-old farm boy named Edward Lee found the instrument while helping his father clear trees by the lake. Champlain's astrolabe eventually made its way into the Canadian Museum of Civilization in Hull, Ontario, where it is now on display.

The journey was not an easy one. Champlain only had two canoes, which could only hold two men each. Both of Champlain's canoes were weighed down with many provisions, weapons, and goods to trade with any Native Americans he might encounter. The journey was made worse when Champlain discovered that de Vignau had made up the story about a passage to Hudson's Bay, causing Champlain to refer to the man in his journal as "the most impudent liar that has been seen for a long time." As if that wasn't enough, Champlain soon encountered a massive waterfall, later named Chaudière Falls, that stood in their way. Champlain and his men had to portage, or carry, all of their equipment and canoes around the waterfall just to continue on.

Later, to avoid the rapids at what is now Gould's Landing, Champlain chose a course through a number of small lakes near Cobden, Ontario, but this route was difficult as well. He and his men continued their journey over an incredible tangle of fallen logs at one particularly difficult point by Green Lake, which is now known as Astrolabe Lake.

As he explored, Champlain did what he could to negotiate with the local tribes for an improved fur trade. Strangely enough, although he was friendly with some of the Native Americans, linguistic (language) abilities were not among his greatest skills. Although he had gained a working knowledge of Spanish when he had sailed to the Gulf of Mexico, he never mastered any of the local languages of New France, and he always relied upon interpreters such as de Vignau, whom he later distrusted.

There was a limit as to how far Champlain could explore with his two canoes, but he did manage to get local Natives to agree to trade fur with the French. Going as far as he could, he eventually had to turn around and go back to the colony. This stay was short-lived, as Champlain decided to head back to France once again, but this time with a business decision in mind.

Chapter 7

Final Years in New France

C hamplain had decided to return to France and form his own trading company. He remained in his home country for two years, but putting his business together may have been only part of the reason he didn't immediately return to

Champlain's final years in New France would be characterized by continuous fighting between Champlain's Native American allies and their enemies.

New France. Family complications also arose when Champlain's wife ran away from both him and her family. While she eventually did return to her husband, the reasons she left were never made apparent. Although Champlain recorded much in his books and journals, he never divulged this personal information.

He also may not have recorded the information because he may not have been part of the resolution, as he left France on April 14, 1615, "with four fathers" (priests) but without his wife, and reached the New World, once again without incident, on May 25.

Once back in the New World, Champlain began a new series of explorations. These included traveling the eastern and southern shorelines of Georgian Bay, an outcropping of Lake Huron, the shores of which he called the Fresh Water Sea, and mapping more of the land around the Saint Lawrence. He seemed to have been determined to see and map as much territory as was humanly possible, whether by canoe or by making his way through the wilderness on foot.

It may have been a realization on Champlain's part that created this urgency, or it might have been that he was simply growing more interested in the well being of the new colonies.

At any rate, Champlain's exploration ended abruptly on August 14, 1615, when he set out at the head of a small band of Frenchmen on an expedition to help the Huron.

The journey through the mostly trackless wilderness of dense forest and rocky terrain took the troop five weeks. The expedition endured many hardships before meeting with its enemy, the Iroquois. The battle consisted of several skirmishes, one of them ending with Champlain near death. Champlain and a band of Huron warriors planned to attack an Onondagas village, but it was well defended with high walls and a moat. Champlain constructed a plan that he thought would turn the tide, involving shields to defend against the villager's arrows and the building of a tower that would get Champlain and his fellow Frenchmen high enough to shoot over the high walls. However, the Hurons did not follow the plan and Champlain was very seriously injured. He was struck twice in the leg by arrows. His injuries must have been incredibly painful, although he wasn't permanently crippled. Champlain wrote with bitter irony, "[The pain] was nothing in comparison with that which I endured awhile I was carried, bound, and pinioned on the back of one of the savages." He was carried by one of the Huron in a makeshift basket and brought safely to a village where he could heal.

While recovering, Champlain did his best to occupy himself by taking notes about all that he saw. He described the Huron and their childrearing techniques, and how they clothed and wrapped the children before tying them to cradleboards, used by many Native tribes in North America.

He wrote, "To adorn the child, they deck the board with beads and put some beads around its neck, no matter how young the baby. Babies sleep between their mother and father at night. The children have great freedom among these tribes; the parents humor them too much and punish them not at all." To Champlain, who was accustomed to the stern discipline common in French households of the time, the Huron children must have seemed unruly.

The battle, in Champlain's eyes, was a failure. The Huron were forced to retreat, and it was clear that the Iroquois had become less fearful of the French muskets.

Champlain, who was not in any condition to return to the French colonies until late that December, had found an old problem was confronting him once again. The merchants who had been supporting the colonies were losing interest in the venture. They were beginning to sound indifferent. Ironically, the problem had arisen through Champlain's own efforts. Because he spent so much time improving the fur trade, it had paid off too well. The business was giving its merchants an immediate profit, but the colony might not show any wealth at all, even after several years. This was because the expenses of the settlement were far

Living with the Huron Tribe

A typical Huron village consisted of rows of houses within a protective wooden palisade. Each house was what is called a longhouse, literally a long rectangle, with slabs of bark covering a framework of wooden poles. The Huron, as well as most of the other tribes of the region, were matrilineal, which means that they traced each family's descent through the mother's side. Each longhouse belonged to a family group and was divided into separate apartments for each family. There were usually ten or more families sharing each structure.

This illustration demonstrates the typical structure of a Huron village, including its protective palisade wall and rows of large longhouses.

greater than the earnings of the seasonal fur trade.

The merchants' lack of enthusiasm meant that Champlain had to make yet another trip to France. He would again attempt to convince the authorities that the colonies must continue to be supported until they were safely self-sufficient. While in Paris, the ambitious Champlain also published another book, titled *Voyages and Discoveries made to New France, 1615–1618*.

Even with this new literary offering as evidence, Champlain had little luck persuading anyone to support the colonies until 1620, when the Duke de Montmorency succeeded de Condé as the governor of New France. The duke seemed much more interested in the colonies than his predecessor, and Champlain, becoming more hopeful that Québec would succeed, finally took his wife with him when he returned to the New World. He also persuaded additional settlers to make the journey to New France, hoping that they could seek fortunes in its expanding fur trade.

Making an Excellent Impression

Madame Champlain must have been shocked when she saw Québec for the first time. After all, she had come from France, the land of fine châteaux (mansions) and refined culture. By contrast, Québec had only a plain wooden fort, muddy dirt streets, and no fine shops or elegantly dressed ladies and gentlemen. It was also a settlement without a theater or cafés, and with very few women. Still, Madame Champlain must have made few if any complaints, at least not to her husband, since there are no records of any in Champlain's detailed journal.

Although she never settled into life in Québec and returned to France in 1624, Madame Champlain must have been a good person. She quickly became well-loved throughout New France, both by the French and the Native peoples. Legend tells of a charming conversation between Madame Champlain and some of her Native women friends. As the story was written, she happened to be wearing a mirror pendant, which was something new to the Native women, as they had never seen a mirror. One of them asked, "Why do I see my face on you?" Madame Champlain replied, "Because you are always in my heart."

The English Attack

By 1625, Québec had finally begun to prosper, expanding beyond its original boundaries. The Duke de Ventadour had become its governor, and he at once began working to further develop the colonies. He also sent over the first **Jesuit** missionaries to aid in converting Native peoples. This was an omen for the tribes that changes to their land were far from over, but a good sign for the colonists since it proved that France was finally serious about their survival and spiritual commitments.

Soon, however, there was an unexpected setback. In July 1628, an English fleet under Sir David Kirk (or, in some accounts, Kirke) and his two brothers suddenly appeared in Québec and demanded a surrender. Champlain's answer was a defiant refusal. The English retreated, but only for the moment.

Québec still relied on European supplies and provisions to satisfy its residents through the winter and into spring. Fleets from France brought nearly everything the residents needed to survive, including flour for bread and staple foods such as beans and peas. Without the French supplies, the colonists would have had to rely largely on a steady diet of salures (salted foods), including cod, cured bacon and beef, and butter. This worried the colonists since, by this point, it was well known that eating such a limited diet was one of the main causes of scurvy.

The Canada Company, which had been organized by Cardinal Richelieu, a powerful figure in the religious and political worlds of France, sent some provisions and more settlers from France, but Kirk captured the ship. Without those vital supplies, Québec spent the winter in great distress. By spring, Champlain knew that there was no other course but to surrender. On July 19, 1629, Québec was under British control and Champlain was taken to England as a political prisoner.

Triumphant Return to Québec

Champlain remained in England for four years. By 1632, England and France had agreed upon the terms in the Treaty of Saint Germain-en-Laye, which stated that Canada, together with Acadia and Cape Breton, would be restored to France. Champlain is credited as being the one to push for the English to return Québec to French control. Champlain was concerned that if the British kept control of Québec and the Saint Lawrence River, they'd have far too much power in Canada. Eventually, the English relented and returned control of Québec and New France to the French. Ironically, that year also saw the publication in France of Champlain's newest books, *The Voyages in Western New France called Canada, written by the Sieur de Champlain during the years 1603 to 1629*, and *Treatise on Seamanship and the Duty of a Good Seaman*.

Champlain was finally a free man and sailed back to New France in 1633. He was immediately reinstated as governor and took possession of Québec again on May 22. Upon his return, he was warmly received by settlers and Native people alike. Now back in Québec, he did everything in his power to strengthen and develop the colony, which numbered about 300 people, a strong population for so young a settlement. He also contacted his Native allies and helped establish a college at Québec in which the children of the Native peoples were taught the French language. Although he didn't want to completely destroy their Native American roots, he did want them to embrace French culture and religion.

While many early European settlers also practiced a singular form of religion, and tried to convert locals to a specific faith, Champlain practiced a more tolerant viewpoint. Perhaps remembering the violence of the religious wars earlier in France, Champlain tried to get the Huguenots and the Catholics to live together in peace in New France. He also seemed to be willing to respect the culture of the Native people, and that allowed the settlers to live peacefully in the New World.

In 1634, Champlain sent a party to found a newer colony, the settlement at what is now Trois-Rivières in Ontario. This colony resulted in the first large-scale immigration of European settlers to Canada.

Champlain never experienced the success of the new settlement. He was no longer the strong, important man and leader he'd once been. The time he spent in England may have weakened him further, and he began believing that his great days of exploration and writing were finished.

Champlain became ill in the fall of 1635. He never recovered, dying of stroke on Christmas Day of that year. It is only fitting that the man who did so much to establish France's permanent position in the New World would be buried in one of the thriving colonies he established. His remains are still in Québec, and the copious number of books he wrote are still available to students and scholars today. Historians continue to read and study the journals of Champlain, learning more about his travels and views on the world of his day.

Although Champlain was forced to surrender Québec to the English in 1629, the colony was restored to France in 1632. Champlain returned to the growing city and spent the last years of his life there.

Timeline

1574

Samuel de Champlain is born in Brouage, France.

1588

The Spanish attempt but fail to conquer England.

1594

Champlain is part of a joint French and English effort against the Spanish.

1599

Champlain sails to the Caribbean and Mexico on his first transatlantic crossing.

1603

Champlain and Pont Gravé set sail from France to explore the Saint Lawrence region in Canada.

1604

Champlain and Sieur de Monts explore the Canadian coast.

1605

Explorations continue as far south as Cape Cod; the first French colony, Port-royal Des Champs, is established near the Bay of Fundy.

1607

The Sieur de Monts's trading monopoly is revoked.

1608

Champlain and Pont Gravé set out on a new mission of settlement; Champlain founds Québec.

1609

Champlain joins the Algonquin people in a raid against the Iroquois; he sees Lake Champlain for the first time and names it after himself.

1610

Champlain is wounded in battle against the Iroquois, this time against one of their forts; he returns to France and weds twelve-year-old Hélène Boullé.

1611

Champlain returns to France, seeking a new sponsor for New France.

1612

The count de Soissons becomes governor of New France, with Champlain as his lieutenant-general.

1613

Champlain returns to New France and the growing colony of Québec; Champlain again searches for the Northwest Passage but fails to find it; the English burn down Port-royal Des Champs.

1615

Champlain interrupts his explorations to fight the Iroquois and is severely wounded.

1620

The Duke de Montmorency becomes governor of New France.

1625

Québec prospers, outgrowing its original boundaries.

1629

Québec is forced to surrender to the British, and Champlain is taken prisoner.

1632

England and France conclude the Treaty of Saint Germain-en-Laye.

1633

Champlain is freed and is welcomed back to Québec.

1634

Champlain founds a new colony at what is now Trois-Rivières in Ontario.

1635

Champlain dies of a stroke on Christmas Day in the city of Québec.

Glossary

Algonquin A related group of northeastern Native American tribes.

astrolabe A navigational device that determines latitude by measuring the angle between the horizon and Polaris, the North Star.

cartographer A mapmaker.

colony A group of people who settle in another territory but keep ties with their native land.

dead reckoning A means of determining a ship's location by measuring as accurately as possible the speed of the ship and the ocean currents, as well as the ship's heading and downwind drift.

hourglass An instrument for measuring time, consisting of two glass chambers connected by a narrow neck and containing a quantity of sand, mercury, or another flowing substance that trickles from the upper chamber to the lower in a fixed amount of time, often one hour.

Huguenots A French sect of Protestant Christians.

Huron A Native American people of northeastern North America.

Iroquois A Native American tribal group; its tribes made up the Iroquois Confederacy.

Jesuit A member of a Catholic order of religious missionaries.

latitude The distance north or south of the equator.

longitude The distance east or west of a generally accepted reference location.

magnetic compass An instrument that uses a magnetized steel bar to indicate direction relative to Earth's magnetic poles.

matchlock gun An early firearm that works by a slow-burning fuse igniting gunpowder.

Montagnais A Native American people who lived in northeastern North America with whom Champlain first allied.

New France The French colonies of continental North America.

New World The European term for the newly discovered lands in North, Central, and South America.

Northwest Passage The term for the theoretical waterway from the Atlantic Ocean to Asia.

paganism Religious practices of someone who is not Jewish, Christian, or Muslim.

Panama Canal The canal that allows ships easy passage between the Atlantic and Pacific Oceans; first opened in 1914.

pelt The skin of an animal with the fur or hair still on it.

quartermaster An ship's officer responsible for the sailors' food, clothing, and equipment.

scurvy A disease caused by a severe lack of vitamin C.

For More Information

Books

Champlain, Samuel de. *Samuel de Champlain: Founder of New France: A Brief History with Documents.* Bedford Series in History & Culture. New York, NY: Bedford/St. Martin's, 2012.

Morganelli, Adrianna. *Samuel de Champlain: From New France to Cape Cod.* In the Footsteps of Explorers. New York, NY: Crabtree Publishing Company, 2005.

O'Brien, Cynthia. *Explore with Samuel de Champlain.* Travel with the Great Explorers. New York, NY: Crabtree Publishing Company, 2014.

Website

The Canadian Encyclopedia's Entry on Samuel de Champlain
http://www.thecanadianencyclopedia.ca/en/article/samuel-de-champlain
Champlain left behind a considerable body of writing, largely relating to his voyages. These works are the only account of the Laurentian colony at the beginning of the seventeenth century.

History of Québec
www.bonjourQuébec.com/qc-en/histoire0.html
Québec boasts a multifaceted geography and diverse landscapes, vegetation and climate. Explore Canada's largest province, its living history, and view slide shows of picturesque scenes.

The Mariner's Museum: Samuel de Champlain
ageofex.marinersmuseum.org/index.php?type=explorer&id=1
This website offers a detailed biography of Samuel de Champlain, accounts of his voyages, and an interactive map.

Index

Page numbers in **boldface** are illustrations.

Acadia, 23–24, 55
Algonquin, the, 33, **36**, 37, **38**, 40, 42
Asia, 5, 20, 21, **34**
astrolabe, 8–9, 47–49

Basque traders, 29, 31–33
Bonne Renommée, La, 17, 26

Cartier, Jacques, 5, **12**, 16, 17, 45
Champlain, Hélène de, 44–46, 50, 53–54
Champlain, Samuel de
  death of, 56
  early life, 6–13
Chaste, Aymar de, 15, 21–22

French and Indian War, 42
Frobisher, Martin, **10**, 21

Gravé, Francis (Pont Gravé), 16–17, 19, 21, 23, 28, 31–33

Hellaine, Guillaume, 11
Henry IV (king of France), 4, 8, 10, 13, **14**, 15, 23, 42, **43**, 45

Iroquois, the, 18, 37, 40–42, 50–51
Iroquois Confederacy, 37–38, 40

Montagnais, the, 34–37, 40–41
Monts, Sieur de (Pierre du Gua), 23, 25–26, 29–31, 33, 43, 45

New England, 25–26
New York, 24, 26, 39
Northwest Passage, 5, 20, 21, **24**, 32, 46
Nova Scotia, Canada, 24–26

Port-Royal, 28–29

Québec, Canada, 5, 9, 16–17,
    30, 33–35, 37, 39–40,
    53–56, **57**

Sainte-Croix, 25
Saint Lawrence River, 16–17,
    20, 25, 27, **30**, 31–32,
    39, 41, 45, 55
scurvy, 25, 35, 54
Spain, 10–11, 13–14, 21,
    29, 32

Tadoussac, 17, 19–21, 23,
    31, 33